The Green Land

JANOSE D. OSEDEME

ISBN: 1535360798
ISBN-13: 978-1535360791

DEDICATION

To the Almighty God.

To all who have made my international student journey a success and have taught me or shown me how to or not to be.

To my family whose life worth of sacrifice has molded me and keeps on shaping me.

CONTENTS

ACKNOWLEDGMENTS

Many thanks to the international students who have contributed in bringing this book to life and who's stories will forever impact coming generations of international students. Alina D'Silva, Chirag Lohiya, Sherina Mutesi, Sean Horsford, Damilola Fola-Owolabi, Abishek Inamdar, Fenose Osedeme, Orn Ngarmcroh, Xinnan Niu, and Bonny Kibuuka, I sincerely appreciate your support and contribution.

Big hugs to everyone at the Penn State International Student's Office who have shown me so much love and support from my first day at Penn State. Anna Marshal with the Global Ambassador Program and Patty Aguilera and Wendy Moynihan with the Global Lion Mentor Program have provided platforms for connecting with amazing people with undeniable and unforgettable impacts on my life.

I specially thank Marcellus Taylor for the great ideas and motivation he continually provides me. Many thanks to Donna Howard for your support. I am glad I can go to her with almost any challenge knowing she will either solve it or find someone else who can.

I really appreciate all my friends and colleagues at Penn State Harrisburg who have helped me adjust and have made my experience in Penn State a fun one.

Special thanks to my beloved sister Fenose, for being my number one fan, supporter, motivator and advisor.

Finally, many thanks to everyone who has taught me or shown me one thing or another and helped me adjust better to the American life; Pastor Tunde Oyelowo, all members of the Living Spring Harrisburg Church and the members of the Lighthouse Club, Penn State Harrisburg.

FORWARD

Making the decision to study in the United States as an international student takes much reflection as well as plenty of courage. Leaving one's support system and everything that is familiar is difficult. As an international student adviser at a major university in the United States, I see the difference that a good support system can make with international students. The mentor/mentee relationship can make a "world" of difference in the academic success of international students. Our Global Lion Mentor program partners returning students (both international and domestic) with incoming international students. We train our mentors on the policy and procedures as well as how to build an effective mentor/mentee relationship. Part of that relationship is sharing stories of what has worked for them and where to find the resources both on campus and in the community, among other things. We have seen great success with this program.

In The Green Land, Janose Osedeme has collected some stories of students who have braved the challenges of being an international student in the United States. These stories help those who are researching being a student in the States by providing insight on how to navigate the challenges of new systems, cultures, relationships, and how to begin to build a new support system.

The United States is a caring and open society that welcomes all. The educational system is second to none. We will continue to attract students from around the globe which benefits not only international students, but also, all students as it provides cultural exchanges and helping all to learn and work in a global society.

I am pleased to write this short introduction for Osedeme's collection of international student stories; and applaud his initiative. I encourage all students to continue to share their stories in an effort to guide those that come after them. In addition to benefiting from the insights of other international students, I advise all international students to reach out to their International Student Support offices at their College or University to ensure they are receiving accurate and concise advice in order to keep their visa status valid.

Best wishes to all, and continue to share your stories!

Donna Howard

Associate Director of Student Affairs

Senior International Student Adviser

Penn State Harrisburg

SECTION 1

1

By
Janose From Nigeria

Coming to America

Nigerians are always very excited whenever they hear about someone who is coming from America or whenever they have the opportunity to go to America. The impression I had when coming to America for the first time was actually very hilarious. I thought white people never needed to use the bathrooms because they were angels, I had thought America was the next best thing to heaven. It was hard to picture what living abroad would look like since I had never experienced such before other than in the movies I had watched. I thought the roads were very perfect and that making money was a piece of cake (by the way it is). Contrary to my beliefs I now see the real America. It is NOT heaven, in fact, it is very far from heaven. It's just more organized than my country Nigeria.

When packing to come to America my mom gave me this really extra-large sweater. She was really bothered about my ability to adjust to the cold because I had never been to America in the winter time. My father gave me a thermal wear and everyone kept asking me to get to warm clothes once I arrived. They'd say "please don't stay outside, please don't go out in the cold, you know it's going to be so cold, blah, blah, blah..." If it was possible my mom would have bundled me up in like 10 clothes but anyway, my thoughts were, "I'll figured it out, It's not a big deal".

When I arrived at the hotel I already reserved, for some funny reason the system refused to accept my card. It kept telling me my card was declined meanwhile I was so sure there was enough money on the card and so I asked them to try the card like a thousand more times but the card refused to work. The lady at the front desk asked me to try another hotel meanwhile the time when she told me to leave was about 10:30 p.m. I tried to leave but after taking about two steps from the front door the cold air slapped me back into the hotel. Once I got back into the hotel I asked to speak with the manager and once the manager came in, we spoke. After a couple of minutes it was agreed that I'd be paying cash. When I got into the room I just drop my luggage fell on the bed and crashed, only to wake up the next morning so hungry, I could have eaten an elephant.

Language Adjustments

The first language in Nigeria is English and I could never have a problem communicating in English or so I thought. On arrival at the campus for the orientation, we were asked to introduce ourselves. I was sure I knew what I wanted to say and that all I had to do was open my mouth and let the words flow out but nah, it wasn't that easy. With benefit of hindsight, I can now tell that I was anxious and apprehensive and that got in my way of expressing myself. I was worried that they might not understand this foreign African accent. My go-to was to try to use an "American" accent to speak. That really complicated my communication because I was pronouncing words how I thought an American would pronounce them without actually knowing how Americans pronounced those words and then the squints on people's faces as they tried to understand what this young man was talking about further heightened my apprehension. I took a couple classes which had students from around the globe. I heard these kids from all over the world speak, I heard even Americans from different parts of the country speak with different accents and they were all well understood. Something clicked right there. They all had accents, if they were understood it was because they were confident in their self-expression and clearly audible. Going forward I decided to be confident, clear and audible when speaking.

Discoveries

›   Americans are very open people, they can be loud at times too.
›   Americans shake very firmly like they intend to squeeze the life out of the other person's hand.
›   Americans too have different accents.
›   Spring comes with the most annoying and repugnant smell of dung. And no its not you who did it ☺ neither did you step on it.
›   Football is not Football here it is Soccer.
›   The weather can be bipolar, be prepared.
›   The weatherman can predict the weather, he can tell exactly when to

expect certain weather and how intense it is going to be. It's not magic, it's science. He is also wrong sometimes.

Weather Drama

I had barely arrived when I went shopping for winter clothing and boots simply because my folks won't let me hear another thing. A day after I bought my winter clothing I was going shopping for groceries when I began to see white flakes falling from the sky. I was so excited to see the snow. I think I stopped to take a picture/selfie, I touched it, I think I might have put a little in my mouth but it was an amazing sight. Walking in the snow was traumatic, for the fear that I will slip and fall. Many people end up with dislocations in the winter. I didn't slip but I almost did regardless of how careful I was.

Cross-Cultural Interactions

I enjoy learning about other cultures and so far, I have learned how to spell my name and say "Hi" in Hindi, Chinese and some other foreign languages. Something I found different was the fact that the Chinese and Indian students like to move together. When Indians speak they use a lot of hand gestures and their heads are always bobbing. That was funny when I first realized it, but I think it's a cultural thing.

Americans can be very loud. For somebody who's coming from a different culture it might be intimidating to see someone constantly shouting in your face. They don't mean any harm, it's just how they are used to speaking.

Americans have very firm handshake that might also be intimidating if you do not understand why this person squeeze your hand so hard. Generally I also discovered that the best way to get around it by making friends and asking questions. If there's anything one doesn't understand it's best to just ask somebody instead of just keeping quiet and hoping that you stumbled on an answer.

I noticed there are some things the Americans wouldn't have a problem talking about, while many times they try to avoid some other topics. On the other hand certain foreign cultures are used to certain greeting styles and they would also consider some topics to be sensitive, meanwhile, an American wouldn't have a challenge discussing that.

Friendships

Attending campus and other social events is a very good way to make new friends. I have made friends with several people I met at social events or campus programs. I think it is important to be open minded and friendly when you are new to an environment. Those new friendships have helped me adjust to my new environment. I still keep in contact with my old friends (thank God for the million social media platforms), but I do not forget to live in the present.

Embarrassing Moment

Since I am a big soccer fan, I attended a school soccer game and was really conspicuous and active throughout the game. It was only after the game was over and I was already on my way back, I realized that I forgot to take off the tag and labels on the new pants I wore. I was so embarrassed.

Also, dressing with the wrong outfit can be so embarrassing. I have learned to wear clothing that matches the weather and season.

Somethings I Wish Americans Knew About Me
> I do not have a pet giraffe.
> The average Nigerian can communicate fluently in English.
> Nigeria is a wonderful place to be. If I am in your country, it is because I need to get better to make my country better.

"….They all had accents, if they were understood it was because they were confident in their self-expression and clearly audible. Going forward I decided to be confident, clear and audible when speaking…."

- J.D. Osedeme

2

By
Alina From India

Coming to America

Initially, leaving my hometown and travelling this far away from family was hard to process for me, but I've always wanted to come to the U.S. My preparation for coming to America involved a lot or researching and inquiring. I had a couple of friends here who I connected with to learn more about the American lifestyle in advance in order to be well prepared with the stuff I needed to pack and bring. I also looked up Facebook and Instagram pages and accounts that would possibly be related to Penn State University, Harrisburg to help me connect with a student or mentor to guide me about the area as well as housing and the weather. Overall, even though it was hard to travel away from my family and my home, I was excited and ready to begin my journey and become independent and responsible.

Language Adjustments

Adjusting to the language here in America was not that hard or complicated for me as I've spoken English all my life, Although, initially, because of the difference in accents it was hard to understand what people were saying. Also, because I was taught British English in school and have been accustomed to it and not American English, adjusting to the different American terms and the difference in the grammar took a while but I'm getting better at it with time and certainly with a lot of practice.

Discoveries

I haven't come across anything shocking except maybe that I adjusted much better than I expected and that the education structure, standard of living and lifestyle of people here in America is amazing. There's always something new to learn every day. Another thing I noticed that amazed me was, there are so many communities and people from different parts of the world here. The diversity is exceptional.

Weather Drama

Adjusting to the weather here has certainly been a struggle. When I first got here, it was hot but bearable considering it was getting close to fall, so it was beautiful. Although when winter started approaching and it started getting cold it was getting tougher to deal with the weather. Also, my experience with summer over here in the U.S. was fun and great, but, the heat was so strong that it would literally drain all the energy out of me.

Housing Drama

When it comes to housing it was never a problem, considering my friends and I already found a great place to live before we got here. The only struggle we had was that the apartment was at a bit of a distance away from campus. There's always a place like the student housing for students to live at as long as they submit an application on time. If not, there are other people renting houses and apartments.

Friendships

Even though it's difficult to interact with people from different cultures because of language restrictions, it's always fascinating to meet people from different parts of the world and from different cultures. After arriving here in the U.S., I have met people from different corners of the world in a very short time and this has helped me learn a lot more about the world. It has been so much fun learning about and being a part of the different cultures and the different festivals, rituals and events celebrated within each culture.

Making new friends was tough in the start because everyone would be with their groups, but, the different events and activities held on campus proved to be a great opportunity to make friends. I also volunteered and joined various clubs which helped me connect with more people, thereby helping me build and grow my friend circle.

Keeping in touch with old friends has probably been the hardest thing to adjust to. Because of having to do everything on my own and having a lot to deal with, like school, clubs, work, chores at home, gym, etc., there's just no time to keep in touch with friends and family. A lot of my friends give me a hard time about it (in a funny way), but we still know we have each other. We catch up every once in a while over text or over skype calls and reminisce about the old days from school. It's really hard to stay in touch when everyone's so busy, but everyone's really understanding of each other's situation as well.

Being miles away from family as stated earlier is certainly the hardest thing to do. But travelling those long hours back home is always worth it. There's no better feeling than going back home and spending time with your family. There's no day that goes by where I don't call my family and spend at least a minute talking to them. It feels sad and upsetting that we're missing out on so many family events and get-togethers but we making up for it when we go back home couldn't make me any happier. It's always a joy of shopping and packing gifts and chocolates for my family when I go back home and spending every moment with them that I may have missed out on.

<u>Something I Wish Americans Knew About Me</u>

› My home culture
› My hobbies
› My obsession with learning more about America and being a part of the American culture.

"....One thing I would love to share from my experience is to always ask questions if you don't understand something. There's always someone who is willing to help out....."

- *A. D'Silva*

3

By
Orn From Thailand

Coming to America

Packing up my stuff was a huge work for me in a preparation process. It took me almost a month. Not only did I have to pick my favorite belongings to bring here, but I also had to clean up my room. My mom told me that I was not going to stay home for years so my room should be functional for my cousins who may visit my mom and stay overnight. I even found some clothes I bought, but I have never used them or used them once. Then, I was able to donate some of my belongings, which was good for me. I know when I come back I will have more belongings.

Language adjustments

Language is a big barrier for me to adjust living in the States. In my country, Thailand, we do not use English that much like some other countries such as India, Singapore, and some countries in Africa, which have English as an official language. I had to take TOEFL preparation course and took the TOEFL test a few times until I met the requirement for the school. Even though they were expensive, I paid for that with my own savings and tried hard because I wished to come here. I would say TOEFL test did not help me with anything here. It was just a score I had to take to meet the requirement. I feel an everyday-English is harder, and it takes time to learn and feel familiar with it.

Weather Drama

I came from a tropical country. So, in my first winter I was so excited about seeing snow for the first time. Moreover, I got to experience a huge snowstorm. I was glad that my Saturday class was canceled due to the weather condition. However, on the day after the snowstorm my aunt told me to shovel the snow that covered my car out, otherwise it would be hard to remove it later. I did not have a shovel, so I had to walk through snow to my friend's house across the street and borrowed his shovel. He also came to help me. It was more tired than I thought. I did not know snow would be that heavy. We had to take turns shoveling the snow. The day after we were sore, and it took a few days to recover.

Housing Drama

My transition to the United States was quite smooth, because I have my uncle and aunt here. They live 3 hours away from my campus. Also, my brother came with me and helped me with getting an apartment. It was an apartment complex, where each room has 4 units. I chose that because I wanted to have some interaction with roommates, especially American to hone my English someway. However, on the first day I walked into my apartment, I was kind of upset. The shared areas were in a mess. One of my roommates was very sloppy, and she left her belongings everywhere. She even had an argument with the other roommate. Luckily, she graduated and moved out in my second semester of staying. However, she left a ton of belongings since she had lived there for almost 4 years. My other roommates and I was so sick of her.

Cross-Cultural Interactions

I like to cook and bake, and I would do it all the time here -- to stay healthy and just for fun. There was one time I made cake rolls for my friends. They were Japanese matcha (green tea) cake with red bean filling. Many of my friends loved it. I brought some to the class, because one of my classmates requested. I found that all of my American friends considered it a weird combination. They said green tea was good, but they have never had red bean in the cake. They could not even finish their pieces of cake. Then, I know now if I want to have my American friends enjoy my cake too, I should make simple flavors like vanilla and chocolate, and make it very sweet.

Generally speaking, Asian and American cultures are very different. There is no wonder that at the beginning, I often experienced culture shock. For example, the first difference I noticed happened when I was in

Washington D.C. waiting for another flight. I walked in to a store at the airport. The staff greeted me and asked me if I would need help. I was thinking that I just wanted to look around. Just leave me alone. Also, I feel people say "have a nice day" all the time. In Thailand we do not say that. We would simply say "good bye".

Friendships

To stay in touch with old friends I use a chat application, LINE on my phone, and I also use Facebook often. I would upload my pictures when I get to travel or have fun activities with friends, so my friends in Thailand can see my life in the United States. I sometimes call them via the LINE application. It is free, but the quality is not great, so we prefer sending messages and pictures. Of course, they all miss me and are waiting for me to come back.

When I first came here, I had a small group of friends. I would stick with my international friends, who I got to know from the new international orientation. In the class, I barely made new friends. I just did not feel comfortable to talk with other people, especially Americans because I was scared that I might not understand what they say or they might not understand me. However, I tried to be involved with all campus activities. It helped me a lot to make new friends, and then I had more confidence to talk with others.

During my first year of staying here in the US, I rarely felt home sick. I enjoyed doing a lot of activities with friends both on campus and off campus. It started after I finished 2 semesters: fall and spring. During the first half of the summer, I was very free. Although I worked part-time on campus and hung out with friends almost every day, I still missed home. I looked at my cat pictures on my phone almost every night. I knew if I were at home in Thailand, she would be always close to me and sleep with me every night. I talked with my brother about that, and he told me I was too free. I should have done something to catch my attention. I began to draw some pictures and read a novel, and then I felt better. I took a class in a second half of the summer. It was a tough class, so I barely missed home again. Now I figured out that being busy would probably be the best way for me to get through homesickness.

Embarrassing Moment

I went to a job fair at the main campus in my first semester. At that time, my English was so bad. I did not want to neglect a chance I had, so I drove there and took some of my Indian friends along. I talked to several recruiters. Talking with the first one was the most embarrassing moment, because I did not understand him clearly and I was so nervous. I also did not know much about his firm, and my future goal was not quite clear.

Somethings I wish these Americans knew about me

> Don't speak too fast with me otherwise you will get asked to repeat many times. I feel familiar with some American accent, but not all. So, please do not get angry when I ask you to repeat.
> I do not like American desserts. They are too sweet, too much calories, and not healthy.
> I seem to be quiet at first but I am not what you thought, I am talkative.

"….I figured out that being busy would probably be the best way for me to get through homesickness…."

-   Orn

4

by
Chirag From India

<u>Coming to America</u>

My name is Chirag Lohiya and I am an international transfer student from India. I am currently a senior undergraduate majoring in Information Sciences and Technology at Penn State Harrisburg and have been here for close to a year. My stay here so far has been mesmerizing and truly amazing. Speaking of my experience, I clearly remember all the hustle that I had to go through on making sure I have all the right documents (like Visa and the I-20), have sorted everything back at my home before leaving and the task of packing all my belongings while traveling to America. Before leaving, I had made sure to meet all my cousins and my friends because I wasn't sure when next we will meet again.

<u>Language Adjustments</u>

English is a universally spoken language and I have been fairly familiar with it, but initially, it was a bit difficult to convey what I had to say to others. I would not say it was tough to cope with the language adjustments as I had taken a number of English proficiency exams before coming here, which made it a lot easier, but sometimes it was a bit difficult to comprehend what the professor was teaching during the lectures and had to really work hard on understanding the way the people spoke, and also, had to improve on my vocabulary. As time went by and as I got to interact with number of people here it became easier transitioning as far as language is concerned.

Discoveries

There were a lot of shocking discoveries that I came across as time went by and honestly some of them were not even what I would have thought of about. The first one being the unlimited soda refill at each and every restaurant. I mean how cool is that? I never would have imagined on having an unlimited soda refill wherever I go.

Another being the concept of fire alarm in houses. I never have had lived in a places with fire alarms around, as a reason, every time I try and cook something, the alarm just goes off.

Further, it is of utmost importance for a person living in America to have a mode of travel, as in, their personal cars, because the places over here are so far from each other that it would take hours to go from point A to B. Also, the fact that a liter of water is more expensive than a liter gas. One of the most shocking discovery was that the people actually do have a sense of responsibility towards their country and they do obey each and every law laid down by the government and because of which I have got to learn a lot about moral responsibilities.

Weather Adjustments

Before coming to America, I have never had the experience of dealing with snow and such harsh weather during the winters. The city in which I resided back home had humid weather almost throughout the year. It was my first experience with snow the last winter, and truly it felt a lot colder than what I had anticipated. To my surprise, the last winter it snowed like it never did before in years and it really made it a lot difficult to bear with the cold weather outside. I remember walking through the snow to the University with boots and all possible winter clothing on, at the same time scared to death to not slip and fall down.

On the contrary, though it was a harsh winter, the experience was not that bad and really enjoyed playing in the snow once the storm had settled. It is not only the winter but the summer is very hot here too. The weather here is a lot extreme with summer being too hot and the winter being too cold. Everything that is said and done it is all worth it and I can finally say that I have managed to get settled over here as far as the weather conditions are concerned.

Cross-cultural Interactions

There are so many students from various countries around the world here with various cultural backgrounds. As far as the American culture is concerned, it is more inclined towards dealing with things practically and welcoming everyone with open hearts.

It is often said that international students in America often find themselves in social situations that elicit stress and anxiety due to cross-cultural differences. But, I believe that stressful social situations can be ameliorated by establishing new friendship and social networks and that is what exactly I have been trying to get myself to do.

Honestly, the cross-cultural interactions have been fun, as the Indian culture is way too different from what the American culture is and is sometimes a bit exhausting trying to explain to my American friends why a certain culture is still prevalent in India.

Friendships

Staying in touch back with friends and family back home is a task as, over here, every individual has to take care of all their stuff on their own, which includes the daily chores too. It consumes almost all of my time leaving very little time for me to talk to my family.

Also, the time zone difference makes it even more difficult as when its morning out here, it turns out to be night back home, and vice-versa. Even after all this I make sure to talk to my family once a day and once a week with my old friends.

My coming to the United States as a student has definitely broaden my horizon about life and knowledge in general. I have gained much confidence and independence than I could have if I stayed with my family in India. This instills in me a sense of achievement and confidence which I never felt in the past. Though being away from family and loved ones is tough, one can find friends for life here. At one occasion a total stranger helped me guide my way back home.

I have made friends with the Americans, and they are as pleasurable as anyone else. They are not at all the way they are perceived in India. I participated in a picnic in an all-American group where, everyone was helpful, and willing to share their knowledge and showed me around. An American has as much sense of culture, religion, and service as any Indian. Although, there are differences in culture and lifestyle, perceptions of disinterest from Americans, language difficulties, academic pressures, preoccupation with study, and cultural stereotypes. At the end it is all worth it!

"….*coming to the United States as a student has definitely broaden my horizon about life and knowledge in general. I have gained much confidence and independence than I could have, if I stayed with my family in India.....*"

\- *C. Lohiya*

5

By
Sherina From Rwanda

Coming to America

I was raised in Rwanda, East Africa. My parents moved to the US. When I was in secondary school (High School) and I had to stay with relatives. In 2010, my siblings and I got our visas to come to the U.S to join our parents we hadn't seen for so long. Everything was happening so fast I didn't even get a chance to say goodbye to my friends.

I remember not sleeping several days before our flight. I was trying to picture how America was going to be and also I was so nervous because I was going to leave my friends, my country, relatives and good food behind. My head was blank for a few weeks because I really didn't know what to think, I didn't have any reactions to being in U.S. People in my country used to say that America is a country full of milk and honey that was basically an expression to show how rich America was.

Language Adjustment

In Rwanda, we speak Kinyarwanda (Native Language), English and French. Growing up I was schooled in the English system from primary to secondary school so I wasn't worried so much about not being able to communicate when I got to the U.S. I thought I knew English well enough to have an actual conversation. The thing was, when I was finally in the US and was attending high school the professors seemed to talk fast and I couldn't understand well. I was actually scared of speaking because I thought no one was going to understand my English since I had an accent. But after a while I got over it and was actually proud of my accent because it made people ask me where I was from and I would have my moment talking about my beautiful Rwanda. Through those discussions I kept getting better and better .

Discoveries

The things that I loved most about America were how people were very helpful and friendly. My parents didn't know much about the school system here so basically our American friends helped us through and made it easier for us to transition. The school was different from the one in Rwanda. I used to attend a boarding school and we stayed in one class and professors had to come to us but here we had to rush to different classes and at times I would get lost but I got used to it. The professors are nice and very helpful which I really like.

I was amazed at how fast food was cheaper than regular food. In Rwanda when you want a burger to pizza. It will cost you a lot so it was amazing to see the difference.

I was also shocked to discover that people here are not as wealthy as I thought when I was back home. My parents used to tell me how in America money doesn't grow on trees. I thought they got easy money; but coming here opened my eyes on how people have to work hard to earn money, and when they do it goes on rent and other expenses.

Weather Drama

The weather, especially snow times were my favorite when I first came. It was my first time seeing the snow. I remember I went sliding and it was so much fun. I was so anxious to see snow, and when it came I was so happy but it didn't last long because it started to be very cold and I started to wish for the warm nice weather. I was amazed to see different seasons and now I loved fall season when the leaves are turning colors it's not hot or cold, just amazing!

Cross-cultural Interactions

Having the opportunity to be in America helped me to have friends from several countries which I would never have done if I was still in Rwanda. These friends bring their cultures and I bring mine and we learn from one another. That way I get to understand them and they understand where I come from. It makes me smile to know that If I go to different countries I will have a friend there, so it won't be too hard. I love testing all the foods from different countries. Being in this diverse place gives me that opportunity to make my taste buds happy.

Friendships

It was hard to talk to my friends because not all of them had technology but the few I got to talk to I had to apologize for not saying goodbyes and we were cool. I stay connected to many of my friends on Facebook, WhatsApp and Instagram.

Embarrassing Moments

My first days in America my parents asked my siblings and I if we wanted to go to McDonalds and we thought they were talking about a person. When we got there we actually saw it was a food place. Another embarrassing moment was when we went to Target and so these doors opened themselves I remember shouting " it's a miracle!" and my parents were laughing. It wasn't that in Rwanda there weren't any automatic doors it's just that I hadn't seen one before.

Somethings I wish Americans knew

I get asked a lot where are you from? And I of course say Rwanda and the follow up comment is always " Hotel Rwanda. Oh yea I saw that movie." The movie is about Rwandan Genocide that happened in 1994. This would make me feel good because at least people know something about where I am from but on the other hand, I wished they knew more about how my country is growing and is just beautiful.

I wish Americans knew that when we come to this country it's not because we don't like where originally come from, but it's because we want better opportunities.

Second, learning a new language is hard and mostly when I talk to someone and they don't seem to understand my accent they have this face they make or they make me repeat it many times which I don't like much. It makes me feel bad about having English as my second language.

Finally, I wish all Americans knew that when they help us international people, it impacts us very much and we are very appreciative. It makes people have a good heart of helping others too. Some of the people who come from different countries and stay here they base on their experience when they arrived and you find them telling you how much they were helped and they want to do the same. So it's like paying it forward.

"....I thought no one was going to understand my English since I had an accent. But after a while I got over it and was actually proud of my accent because it made people ask me where I was from and I would have my moment talking about my beautiful Rwanda...."

-   Sherina

6

By
Sean From Grenada

Coming to America

Leaving your country to settle in another country is never easy. There are so many things one will have to adjust to in order to make themselves comfortable and to be able to mesh with the people living there. Transitioning from one culture to another takes time effort and energy. Some of these basic changes include food, clothing, language and the mannerisms of the people. Apart from that, separating from your family and loved ones is difficult. These things might sound simple, but in my preparation before leaving Grenada to study in the United States, these were the things I feared the most.

The first place I landed and explored in the United States was New York City. I couldn't help but notice the difference in the way people got along with each other on the streets. Everyone seemed to be about their business and never said hello to the person passing next to them. On the other hand, island people would never pass anyone on the road without saying hello. I guess it's because the island's population is so small that everyone relates like family. Growing up with this tradition instilled in me, it was only natural for me to the same in the big city, only to quickly realize that things were quite different and not many persons responded to my greetings. In fact, I received a few stares that almost led me to believe I was crazy. I was told that life in the big city could be very impersonal and cold; however experiencing it firsthand made me very uncomfortable. Being the naïve person I can be at times, I also tried the same thing when I arrived at Penn State Harrisburg, but only later learned that this was a norm.

Language Adjustments

Although I am from an English speaking country, it was still difficult at times to communicate with the American students, simply because we use different slang and words within our sentences. Not only do we have a dialect, we also speak very fast. This of course did not make it any easier for me to communicate with them. The key, however, is to always be conscious of the words you're using and slow down as much as possible while trying to be as clear as you can. This will definitely help overcome the language barrier, especially if you're from a country that speaks a different language.

Weather Adjustments

Living in America gave me a greater appreciation for the warm climate in the Caribbean. Coming from the islands where the temperature is 80 degrees year round, I was very much excited to experience my first winter. It was like a dream awaiting to finally become a reality.

The first time I saw snow I couldn't restrain myself from playing in it. Whether it was making snow balls or building a snow man, I did it all. It was not long before I realized that the winter is not as appealing as I expected once it began to get colder. Nothing seemed to be able to keep me warm enough. My eyes were constantly running and my nose will always be stuffy.

Walking to and from school was the most uncomfortable experience, especially when the wind was blowing freezing cold air straight at you. I couldn't wait for it to be over. Not only was I bothered by the cold, but I lost count of the many times I got frost bite in my toes and almost broke my limbs falling on what is called "black ice". After my first experience of winter, it instantly became my most hated season in America. There was one good thing about it though and that was the fact that classes always got canceled once it snowed heavily enough.

Cross Cultural Interactions

The American culture is very diverse because of the many different types of people living there. As a result of cultural penetration, I noticed that some of things we have adapted to in Grenada are very similar to what I've seen while studying in America. However, so many Americans are deeply embedded in their own culture and have very little knowledge of the outside world. I wish Americans knew a lot more about my culture, hence the reason I am always eager to show pictures and clips of what is like living on an island. Especially the food we eat, the way we dance and the cultural activities we engage in, just so we can better understand each other and be able to better relate to each other.

Friendships/Family

Some of my international friends to date complained about how difficult it was to make friends. That is so true because Americans can be very unfriendly to people they don't know. However, what I found to be very helpful was getting involved in different clubs and groups. This can really help you to make friends since you will be interacting with different students from different countries including students from America.

Making the right friends was always priority to me because it is important that you know and understand the different the cultures in order to be able to effectively relate to other students. This goes especially for American students because they are the ones that would know the most about their cultures and if you are interested in understanding and relating to them, the best way to do so is through making friends.

Finally, leaving your country, family and loved ones behind is never easy. The first couple of months would be the toughest as you're still adjusting to a new environment with no friends nor family to help you to do so. As long as you keep on pushing forward and remain resilient, everything eventually falls into place and once you start making friends and settling into your new environment it eventually would start feeling closer to what a place called home should feel like.

"….I wish Americans knew a lot more about my culture, hence the reason I am always eager to show pictures and clips of what is like living on an island. Especially the food we eat, the way we dance and the cultural activities we engage in, just so we can better understand each other and be able to better relate to each other….."

- *Sean*

7

By
Abishek From India

Coming to America

Well, I was enrolled in an undergraduate transfer 2+2 program, so, I was mentally prepared for coming to America. My few family members were here, therefore, I got good guidance on how to prepare for the trip.

Everyone knows that getting here is not at all easy because of the visa requirements. I made the list of things to bring, so that I don't miss anything.

Language adjustments

My mother tongue is not English. Although my high school and junior college education was in English, I was not very confident about it. After coming here, initially I faced a lot of difficulties in understanding the language. I got hang of it later.

Most shocking discoveries

One of the most shocking things I noticed here was the mannerism of people. People here are so polite, humble, and helpful. I automatically got that habit.

Just to mention - When I went back to my home country for vacation, all of my family members and friends told me that I have become more mannered person. Well perks of living in this country ☺!!

Weather drama

What should I say about the weather? Man, it's very cold here. Being from a tropical region, it was very difficult for me to adjust to the cold. I used to wear layers of clothing. But if there is severe cold and windstorm, then layers of clothing also wouldn't be enough. But I enjoyed the snow. It was just amazing.

Cross-Cultural interactions

I didn't face much difficulty in getting along with the people here, but, I would say that initially I faced difficulties while talking to new people. Many things come to play here, such as language, lifestyle, culture, background, and mindset. So, it is not always easy to get along, but we can definitely get along with the people if we take the lead and initiate a conversation. People here are so friendly and open-minded.

Friendships

I'm still in touch with my old friends. I think we should never disconnect from old friends. They are the ones who supported us to come here. I keep in touch with them via Facebook, WhatsApp, etc.

Most embarrassing moment

I don't know the most embarrassing moment, but I had one moment when I slipped on the ice during the winter. Everybody was watching and laughed. That was fun though.

Family

My family is very supportive. I talk to my parents on Skype whenever I get the time. This way every one of us feels like we are close to each other. Technology really helps to maintain relationships.

"....it is not always easy to get along, but we can definitely get along with the people if we take lead and initiate conversation ...."

-   *A. Inamdar*

8

By
Xinnan From China

Coming to America

I got much useful information for packing and preparing from the internet. There were a lot of students who had finished their process and then shared and posted their experience on some community, like Reddit.

Language adjustments

Even though I took TOEFL and GRE exams, and got the grades which were qualified for graduate school, I didn't know how to do the daily life conversations with people. At the beginning, I could not understand what people were talking about because they were speaking too fast or I just did not know the words that they were using in the sentence. I was not brave enough to stop people and ask them to speak slowly. So I did lots of work after class. I took an online English class from my country to improve my accent.

My roommate gave me a lot of compliments on my improvements which made me more confident than before. She also gave me some advice on increasing my vocabulary. For listening, I fell in love with YouTube videos, I have a favorite YouTuber, and I watch his videos every day. Sometimes, I repeat the same video again and again.

Discoveries

The most shocking discoveries is that I should keep and fight for my own benefit. Because we were taught that the benefit of collective organization is much more important than a person's benefit and people should sacrifice their own benefit when there is a conflict between the organization and a person.

Weather drama

I grew up in Northeastern China, and I love the winter and so the weather is not a problem for me. But the weather here is quite different with the one in my hometown. It will never rain during the winter in my hometown.

Housing drama

I was lucky that I have two great roommates. We have same habits and living style. They are also very nice to me. We went to dinner together, watched Korean drama together and had a small intelligent party together.

Cross-Cultural interactions

The American Culture is different from the Chinese culture, or I can say the western culture is different from the eastern culture. I haven't gotten many chances to have connections with American students, but I learned from my few interactions with American students that it can be hard for me to be one of them.

Friendships/Family

Making new friends can be easy if you go to a lot of events and activities. Being brave to talk to different people and showing respect to different cultures can be really helpful.

It's hard to keep in touch with old friends from my country. Sometimes, I had a problem that I want to talk with them, and they just could not understand my situation because they don't have the experience of study abroad. And also because of time difference, I couldn't get a reply from them immediately. But I still keep updating them about my experience.

I don't miss my family that much. But I really missed my family when I was sick or was in a very tough situation.

Most embarrassing moment

I didn't know how to be polite when I was asking for help from someone. Once I wanted to ask for a time card from an assistant. I should have said "Can I have a time card?" but I said "I want a time card." I did not realize I was being rude to say that until the assistant showed her emotion by dropping her mug on the desk. That was my most embarrassing moment.

Somethings I wish Americans knew about me

> The things that I wish Americans knew are not about me as a person but about my country and my culture. I did not have much unhappy experience with Americans, but I did hear a lot from other Chinese students.

> I wish they knew how to show respect to people from other culture and know internationalization cannot be avoided. Every aspect of your life is influenced by that.

> Lastly if you have a chance, please visit my country, you will know it's different from the one that you learned from media.

"....For *listening, I fell in love with YouTube videos, I have a favorite YouTuber, and I watch his videos every day. Sometimes, I can repeat the same video again and again* ...."

-     Xinnan

9

By
Bonny From Uganda

Coming to America

I was born and raised in Wakiso, Uganda. On 07/04/14, God opened doors for me to move to the United States of America to start my journey of becoming a pilot. I was super excited that I was starting to live the dream, but I was sad too because I was leaving my family. So when I was packing to leave I was experiencing winter and summer at the same time (happiness and sadness)

Discoveries

When I got to the States, I landed at LAX in California. I was first shocked by the cars, buildings, people, huge airports and planes because that was always my dream. As I continued to many other different States, I started to discover many other things like, these guys are not ashamed of farting in public like it is in Uganda. It's actually funnier if they can produce a better sound with their farts. Oh boy!!

Language adjustments

At the very beginning, I sucked at my communications because people wouldn't understand my accent; neither could I understand everything they say, so I would find myself saying the Hmm and yes often. (DON'T LAUGH!!!). The other thing was the use of words, in Africa there are some words we say and we look at them as normal words but it's a big deal in the States if you use them. I confess to have used a lot of the S - word while playing soccer, but it was just that I didn't know it was a big deal here.

Weather drama

It wasn't a big deal when I lived in the south (Alabama) till I moved to the flight school in Michigan, one of the coldest states in America, whenever it snowed and I think it's too much, my friends would say "it is not yet there, wait until tomorrow" and that's how I lived through the winter season. All I could pray for was to get to summer soon. I was freezing.

Housing drama

I never had any big issues with the housing here, actually I love the houses here. I usually slept well always. One thing I noticed here was, if you visited someone and they don't have enough beds the visitor would sleep on the couch. But in Africa I think the hosts would sleep on the couch and the visitor gets the bed. (Hahahahaha African pride!).

Friendships/Family

It wasn't hard for me to make friends here because most of my friends I met at soccer games, and others just wanted to know more about Africa where I come from. And that kind of affected my old friends back in Uganda. The other thing was the time differences it wasn't easy to keep up most of my friends because as I sleep they would be waking up and vice versa. But I did keep up with most of them.

My family has been so loving, they are all back in Africa and we don't often communicate because it's kind of expensive to call them daily, due to high costs of living here.

Something I wish Americans knew about me.

I think Americans should know that I am a strong fighter, I am not intimidated about anything. Coming from a 3rd world country doesn't mean we can't do anything.

"….I would like Americans to know that I am a strong fighter and I am not intimidated about anything. Coming from a 3rd world country doesn't mean we can't do anything….."

-   *Bonny*

10

Damilola From Nigeria

<u>Coming to America</u>

This was pretty normal for me. My parents packing all the bogus sweaters they could find for me and telling me to keep warm like I would expose myself. The interesting part came when I got here. My roommate wasn't around and she wasn't okay with sending me the keys to the apartment so I had to find a motel to stay. I don't know why I found a motel at that was a $35 Uber trip away from school, but I did anyway. I was just trying to find the cheapest place and Budget-Inn came up, so I took it. I got there on a Tuesday and there was no way I would have just sat in the room from Tuesday till Sunday. There was also no way I would spend $70 on the Uber ride everyday so my friend suggested I take a cab to downtown and take a bus from downtown to school, and vice-versa for my return trip. That saved me money, but standing in the cold waiting for the bus to come wasn't the most pleasant experience.

<u>Language Adjustment</u>

I have no problem hearing people, but everyone says I talk too fast. One time someone even offered to give me a Spanish interpreter. I got warned by family that were already here that I would have to talk slower but I didn't think it will be an issue. Still working on the talking slowly part though.

Discoveries

That the first day of spring smelled like poop lol. I remember that day clearly. I was almost late for my bus, so I had to run to of the house. I couldn't stop wondering if I had stepped on a cat or dogs poop since the smell seemed to follow me everywhere. Wasn't until after I asked a friend and I was told it was manure people used for planting that I stopped sniffing myself.

Another thing that amazed is how nice the people here are. There was a fire incident at my apartment and the help and care I received from the community was overwhelming. Like I got random people calling me and offering to give me food, clothes and furniture. At some point I had to start avoiding our international student advisor because all she ever did was try to give me stuff.

Weather Drama

Before I came here I always thought I would have a brain freeze because of the cold. That didn't happen though and I handled the weather quite well except for one not so great experience. I went to Walmart and got dropped like 10 mins from my apartment. I had a lot to carry and I didn't have my gloves on. When I got home that day, my fingers were freezing. I was so scared I thought they would fall off. Luckily for me they didn't fall off. Well I learned a big lesson that day and never left my house without gloves.

Friendship/Family

Making new friends wasn't easy when I got here. But after a while I started meeting people through my Church and the various events the international office at Penn State Harrisburg organized.

Time difference and grad school work load hasn't really helped, but I try my best. I don't communicate with everyone I used to but I'm blessed to have a couple of friends that are understanding.

I miss my family so much, but I speak to them at least once a week so that keeps me happy.

Somethings I wish Americans knew about me.

I only have one thing: The official language of my country is English so I can speak English and if that doesn't convince them that my English is good, the fact that I couldn't come here without passing the TOEFL exam should be proof enough.

"….*Making new friends wasn't easy when I got here, but after a while I started meeting people through my Church and the various events the international office at Penn State Harrisburg organized…..*"

- *Damilola*

SECTION 2

Practical Solutions

International students are an adventurous and courageous set of people who have left their homes in search of a better life and better opportunities abroad. It takes courage for international students to leave the life they had, all they have known to be home and family to migrate to a somewhat uncertain future.

It takes a great deal of boldness resilience and determination to be successful as an international student. This is simply because the hurdles the international student has to overcome on the journey to success abroad can be said to be three times much more than fellow students from that country.

Fears and uncertainty about what the future holds and what might become of the international student sometimes can be overwhelming. If the international student is not prepared mentally for the life abroad, falling into depression is most likely.

The international student battles with the following issues which we will explore and proffer practicable solutions.

- Financial Aid
- Weather
- Friendships
- Transportation
- Language adjustments
- Culture Shock

- Housing
- Educational Style Differences
- Food
- Religion
- Visa Status

Financial aid

The topic of financial aid is very crucial to international students. Many international students arrive on campus with a lot of questions bothering on financial aid and when those questions are not adequately answered it can cause some unrest for the international students.

The reality about availability of the financial aid to international students compared with the indigenous students can be expressed in a ratio of 2:9. That is, for every 9 financial aid available, most likely there will be 7 available to indigenous students and 2 or less available to the international students. This is not to shoot down the hopes of getting a scholarship, it only highlights the competitive nature of aids available to international students.

Band Aid
›   Consult with the campus about financial aids available
›   Search online for organizations that grant financial aids to students
›   Seek on-campus jobs
›   For graduate students, Teaching Assistants and Graduate Research Assistant can be available
›   In the absence of any other option, student loans may be an alternative.

<u>Weather</u>

Adjusting to the weather can be such a herculean task. International students coming from various kinds of weather to a different weather climate experience some form of disorientation at first. Sometimes they discover that the weather is more severe than they had prepared for and some other times it isn't as horrible as they had thought.

On arrival they find that some other students either have skimpy clothing on in the cold or have too much off during the summer. These clothing styles may be considered fashionable and so they find the feel the pressure to dress like that even though they are inappropriate for the particular weather. Sometimes they find the weather bipolar and it may seem that they have more than one season in the same day or week. This can cause some disorientation.

<u>Band Aid</u>
›   On arrival, international students should endeavor to get adequate clothing and shoes for the appropriate weather condition.
›   Trust the weatherman 85% of the time
›   Check the weather forecast for the day and even the week ahead of time.
›   Don't dress the way others dress just to fit in. They have been in the cold or heat (as the case may be) all their lives. Dress so that you are comfortable either in the cold or heat.
›   Dress in layers. Summer time can be very hot outside but quite chilly inside with the air conditioning on.

☐

Friendships

Hard as it may be to move on and make new friendships, it is very important. Friendships with other international students as well as indigenous students is important. Friendships with other international students helps the student to have a rounded understanding of the world they live in. It broadens the horizons of the international student as well as helps them to learn about other cultures around the world. It helps the student to experience other countries' cultures without actually traveling there.

Friendships with indigenous students helps the international student in many ways.
› It helps the international student to pick-up/understand common terms used in communication (slangs)
› It helps the international students to adjust better to the culture

Due to the fact that friendship is very important it must also be treated with care and caution. It is important for the international students to make friends with people who will help them achieve their goals. Friendships made should add value and not erode values. As those who are not going in the same direction cannot hold hands, so also friendships should not be made with people who will not help in achieving the goals and aspirations of a successful life.

Many international students go abroad at an age where they are just finding out who they are and understanding themselves and so this makes them more prone to negative influence.

Band Aid

›   As it is said "He who wants to have friends must first himself be friendly".
›   Attend social events and school events.
›   Meet new people with a mind that is open to learn
›   Make friends with people who add value to you
›   Be proud and willing to share and show off your culture to people
›   Remember, those going in different directions cannot hold hands.

Language adjustments

Uncertainty about how foreigners will perceive the international student's accent is another big challenge. In order to be accepted into the program, most times the program will require international students from countries that do not speak English to take English proficiency examinations. Only when the student satisfactorily passes those proficiency exams will they be accepted into the programs they applied for.

It is thus very important for the international student to remember that they have put in efforts to learn the language and have satisfactorily passed the required proficiency examinations and therefore they are be able to communicate in that language. All that is needed is practice in order to perfect speaking and writing in English language.

Band Aid

› Practice speaking English language and do not hide among friends from the same nationality among whom you feel safe to speak your home language
› Make use of the learning centers or language aid facilities on the campus
› Online resources are available for spellchecking
› Do not be shy to ask colleagues for help.
› Watch TV and Movies in English language.
› Remember: "Practice makes perfect".

Culture Shock

Culture shock according to the Wikipedia is

"Culture shock is an experience a person may have when one moves to a cultural environment which is different from one's own; it is also the personal disorientation a person may feel when experiencing an unfamiliar way of life due to immigration or a visit to a new country, a move between social environments"

Culture shock is the cause of most home-sicknesses experienced by international students. Due to the many social media platforms now available to connect with friends, it is easy to keep up with friends and family abroad. When many students arrive abroad and find the experience very different they fall back to the friends and family they left back home for solace. This makes the time it takes them to adjust to the new culture even longer. The longer the period of adjustment the more the probability for home sickness.

Band Aid
› Keep up with friends and family but not so frequently that it affects the time you should spend getting to know your environment.
› Go out, meet new people with an open mind. A mind that accepts the difference and is willing to learn from them.

Transportation

Getting around for international students may seem to be a big challenge with the different transportation options available. If you don't own a car, you may find mobility to be a herculean task. Nonetheless, the solution is to get familiarized the available transportation system around you. This is important because the United States of America is a relatively big country and all 50 states have different kinds transportation services.

While getting around within your school environment, you may need to take advantage of the School's shuttle. For areas outside the school's vicinity, it is possible to use the local community's public transportation.

If you decide to get a car, you will need to get a driver's license and proper registration for the car. It is important to keep the vehicle registration papers up to date. Many times students forget to update the inspection stickers.

For long distances and interstate travel, the rail system (e.g. Amtrak), bus transportation (e.g. Greyhound or Mega bus) or air travel can be used. It all depends on how much time and money you're willing to spend.

Band Aid
›   Know your area
›   Plan your route before the day
›   Ask questions, and do your research prior to taking any trip.
›   Use technology. Example: google maps, map quest to prevent you from getting lost
›   Get a valid driver's license.
›   If you are getting a car, properly register your car at the State Department of Motor Vehicles(DMV).
›   Get the car inspected and keep the inspection updated.

Education style differences

One very peculiar difference in the American educational system is the mode of instruction. For international students, this new mode of teaching may contribute to the culture shock. In order to overcome challenges and adapt properly, it is important to be open to change and learn to utilize all the resources available within your school.

In most developing countries and underdeveloped countries, despite the increase in globalization, the mode of education is still mostly via the classroom. In most institutions here in the US, there is a prevalence of virtual (online) education and some international students may need further tutoring on how to use these online platforms.

For any international student, it may be surprising to find out how much writing is required in the American educational system. Some other shocking discoveries may include metric system used and the type of English language used. Students from countries colonized by the British use the British English while communicating (writing and oral). On the other hand, the United States uses the American English. The differences occur in the spelling of words for example in the use of "s" and "z" as in organisation (British) and organization (American).

Band Aid
> Be proactive
> Make relevant friendships that will help your academics
> Embrace new technology
> Know your professors – Understand their requirements for the course
> Use your school's resources like the library (everything you need is probably in the library), writing centers, tutors etc.

Food

The type of food or dieting options available to international students are really important for their adjustment process. This is because food in some sense helps us find some comfort or familiarity with what we're used to, back at home. It is not surprising to find out that initially some international students may have trouble adjusting to the food available. The key is to do a lot of research. Eat what you feel comfortable with, while you adjust to an entirely new option.

It is often said that America is a melting pot, and students will find this especially true in the variety of food and meals that are available in the US from other countries and cultures. Most large communities have international stores, but in smaller towns and cities, it is advisable to start out with a more intercontinental and widely known option, like chicken.

Band Aid
›   Do some research.
›   Plan meal if possible and be disciplined
›   Learn new health eating habits
›   Preparing your own meal is always cheaper and healthier than eating out

Religion

America is a place of diverse cultures, religions and faiths and so religious adjustment cannot be overlooked when discussing the transition of international students to the American culture.

It is important that the international student feels safe and comfortable to practice their religion in order to have a smooth transition. Connecting with people of similar faith can help the international student feel comfortable and safe to practice their faith.

Band Aid
› Ask questions
› Do your research
› Learn to tolerate others of different faiths
› Stay positive and have an open mind.

Housing

As it is for any individual, housing contributes to one's sense of security. Having a sense of security will help the international student to adapt properly to the new environment, it will also aid the development of essential skills and competencies for academic success. The quality of their physical environment will have a significant impact on how students are able to interact, build relationships and cope with the academic requirements

Finding a suitable housing option may take a lot of time and research. Types of housing options for students include; shared houses, flats, units or apartments, on-campus accommodation by colleges and off-campus purpose-built accommodation. Some international students are from large communal families while others have lived in smaller settings. It is advisable to pick an option most convenient and suitable for your individual needs.

Band Aid

> Ask your school's housing department for assistance.
> Ask a lot of questions when unsure, be aware of lease agreements and fine prints in contracts.
> Consider the factors of safety, proximity to classes and other relevant locations when choosing a housing option.
> When choosing a roommate be sure to communicate, set boundaries and basic agreements in order to avoid conflicts.

Visa Status

Maintaining a current/valid visa status is very important for international students. The ability to continue studying and making progress and enjoying the life in the United States hinges on the visa status. It is no good to have good grades and all the successes desired but be unable to continue studying because of a visa issues.

While there are different types of student visas; F1, J1 etc., being updated about the requirements and regulations governing the type of visa we hold is our responsibility. Employment rules for these visa types vary and must be strictly adhered to.

OPT (Optional Practical Training) and CPT (Curricular Practical Training) are the possible employment authorizations for international students in America. International students can work on their campuses without any authorization from the U.S government.

Band Aid

> Ask your school's international student department for information/clarification.
> You can search online for information from the USCIS website regardless of whether your school has or doesn't have an international student office.
> Keep updated on the rules governing your visa in terms of employment or otherwise.

NOTES

Made in the USA
Middletown, DE
26 August 2021

46918874R00038